Snout

Written by

Simon Puttock

Illustrated by

Thomas Docherty

OXFORD

UNIVERSITY PRESS

OXFORD
UNIVERSITY PRESS

Great Clarendon Street, Oxford, OX2 6DP, United Kingdom

Oxford University Press is a department of the University
of Oxford. It furthers the University's objective of excellence
in research, scholarship, and education by publishing
worldwide. Oxford is a registered trade mark of Oxford
University Press in the UK and in certain other countries

Text © Simon Puttock 2015
Illustrations © Thomas Docherty 2015

British Library Cataloguing in Publication Data
Data available

ISBN: 978-0-19-835637-0

10 9 8 7 6 5 4

Paper used in the production of this book is a natural, recyclable product
made from wood grown in sustainable forests. The manufacturing process
conforms to the environmental regulations of the country of origin.

Printed in China by Leo Paper Products Ltd

Acknowledgements

Series Advisor: Nikki Gamble

Every morning, Snoot
woke up feeling worried.

"What if the sky falls down?" said Snoot.

"What if I step on a
crack in the pavement?"

"Oh dear," said Snoot. "What if two stripes aren't *enough*?"

"What if something terrible happens?"

"Snoot," said his friend Milton, "you worry too much."

But one night, something terrible *did* happen.
Something terrible tapped at Snoot's bedroom door.

"Snoot!" it boomed.

"I'm your **big bad** dream and I am going to **get** you!"

Snoot hid under
the covers all night.

"Dreams can't *hurt* you, Snoot," said Milton.

"But Milton, it was terrible," said Snoot. "And horrible. And dreadful, too!"

"If it comes back, you must chase it away," said Milton.

"I can't do that," said Snoot. "It's too scary!"

The next night, the big bad dream was waiting at the top of the stairs.

"Snoot!" it boomed.

"I am going to get you!"

Snoot hid in the downstairs bathroom until morning.

"Next time," said Milton, "say this.
*Go away, you big bad dream and
do not dare come back again!*
That should do the trick."

"Oh!" cried Snoot. "I can't say
that! I'm not brave enough."

That night, Snoot was about to eat his tea when the big bad dream came creeping in.

"Snoot!" it boomed.

"I am going to **get** you!"

Snoot didn't stop
running until he got
to Milton's house.

"Snoot," said Milton sternly. "You must make this dream go away. If you don't, you will be stuck with it forever!"

"*Forever?*" howled Snoot. "Oh no!"

"Don't worry," said Milton. "Next time I will help you to be brave."

That night, the big bad dream came
creeping in once again.

Then the big bad dream saw Milton.

"*Yikes!*" said Milton, and he hid behind the sofa.

But Snoot did not say "yikes".
Snoot did not hide behind the sofa.
Suddenly, Snoot felt very cross.

14

"How *dare* you scare my friend like that!"
Snoot shouted. "You're not *Milton's* dream!
You are *my dream* and

          I will not let you scare him."

Just like that, the dream
began
to
shrink!

"And because you are *my* dream, you will do what
I say!" said Snoot.

The dream shrank a bit more.

"And *I* say, **go away**,
you big bad dream
and do not dare
come back again!"

Snoot's dream shrank to the size of a potato.

In a tiny voice it said, "I'm really very sorry."
And then it vanished.

"Snoot," said Milton, "you bravely *saved* me!"

"Yes!" said Snoot happily.
"I suppose I *did!*"

When Snoot woke up
the next morning,
he felt different.

He did not feel worried, he felt good.

"Hello," he said to himself in the mirror. "I like your stripes!"

The Snoot in the mirror grinned back at him.

It was raining.

"Goodness, the sky *is* falling," Snoot thought.
"I shall need an umbrella."

Then he went out and stepped on a pavement crack ...

... and guess what?

Nothing terrible
happened at all!